Seasons
—— *of* ——
Consciousness

Seasons
—— *of* ——
Consciousness

MARTINA W. MULLINS

AuthorHouse™
1663 Liberty Drive
Bloomington, IN 47403
www.authorhouse.com
Phone: 1-800-839-8640

© *2013 by Martina W. Mullins. All rights reserved.*

No part of this book may be reproduced, stored in a retrieval system, or transmitted by any means without the written permission of the author.

Published by AuthorHouse   03/18/2015

ISBN: 978-1-4918-3041-3 (sc)
ISBN: 978-1-4918-3042-0 (e)

Library of Congress Control Number: 2013919117

Print information available on the last page.

Any people depicted in stock imagery provided by Thinkstock are models, and such images are being used for illustrative purposes only.
Certain stock imagery © Thinkstock.

This book is printed on acid-free paper.

Because of the dynamic nature of the Internet, any web addresses or links contained in this book may have changed since publication and may no longer be valid. The views expressed in this work are solely those of the author and do not necessarily reflect the views of the publisher, and the publisher hereby disclaims any responsibility for them.

CONTENTS

DECEPTION 1
I WON'T FALL 2
WE LEARN 3
YOU LOSE 4
JOURNEY 5
CRY OF THE HEART 6
AWAY 7
WINTER 8
ACCUSED 9
Bêtise 10
SPRING 11
GUILT IS BORN 12
LONGED 13
MY INNERMOST 14
MY DEAREST CHILD 15
HATE 17
STORM 20
JUST ME 21
CRYSTAL FOREST 22
IN DUE TIME 23
SUMMER 24
FANTASIES 25
UNDERSTANDING 26
ANGER 27
MAY NEVER BE 28
CONFIDENCE 29
SECRET ADMIRER 31
RUNNING 32
PROCLAMATION 33
CANDLELIGHT 34
AUTUMN 35
FATE 36
FRIENDSHIP 37

TROUBLED WATERS	38
BROKEN PROMISE	39
BELIEVE	40
LOVE ME	41
MIRAGE	42
WILD CHILD	43
DEPRESSION	44
A DOG'S LIFE	45
A CAT'S HUNT	46
IMMATURE HEART	47
GREED	48
PREDETOR	49

DECEPTION

The genuine love we hold,
devoured in passion to unfold.
Wandering eyes of your lust,
my affection you've unjust.

I dread of your digression,
of your impulsive obsession.
The deception of man's desire,
conscious of playing with fire.

My own devotion, your demise,
the lost trust of spoken lies.
My agony grew into hate,
for my heart you betrayed.

Martina W. Mullins

I WON'T FALL

Regardless the disappointment,
I won't dwell, I won't drown.
Yearning for contentment,
because I won't fall down.

No matter the failure,
my happiness will not frown.
I will maintain composure,
because I won't fall down.

My self-healing vitality,
I wear like a crown.
Brave for me to be,
because I won't fall down.

WE LEARN

We learn to listen,
when others speak.
We learn to give,
When others need.
We learn to trust,
when there aren't lies.
We learn to forgive,
when others apologize.
We learn to love,
when they show themselves.
We learn to respect,
when others help.

YOU LOSE

Seasons have come and gone,
wasted are all my fights.
Sleepless I reach the dawn,
conquered the callous nights.

Guilty as you've become,
of your rotten game.
Recognizing before long,
I have you to blame.

Once again you lose,
stronger I will become.
Your neck in the noose,
returning where I'm from.

The devil's laughter you hear,
everlasting burning in hell.
Your judgment day is near,
in your conviction you'll dwell.

JOURNEY

Feeling the cold rain,
on my warm face.
Walking the dirt path,
a new journey I embrace.

Troubled by fear,
of the unknown.
Waiting until time,
becomes my own.

In your eyes I see drive,
making me feel so alive.
You're holding my hand,
guiding me to the end.

Martina W. Mullins

CRY OF THE HEART

Tears falling in the rain,
I'm wrenched with grief,
as I wander into exile,
I lose my belief.

One broken heart of two,
as it bleeds once more.
Sorrow remains my enemy,
invading my very core.

AWAY

Each day I think of you,
envision your sweet smile.
Longing to be with you,
remembering you worthwhile.

Even though we're far apart,
our love remains strong.
I'll keep you in my heart,
to each other we belong.

Many miles you are away,
some day we reunite.
Dreams from the other day,
I go over every night.

Martina W. Mullins

WINTER

Snow has fallen from the night before,
a white blanket glistening in the morning rays.
Children anxiously dashing out the door,
from the hilltop a sleigh ride chase.
Christmas trees adorned in silver and gold,
ornaments shimmer in the candlelight.
Families are gathered of young and old,
sitting by the fire of the wintry night.

ACCUSED

Accused of something,
nothing has become.
Pointed fingers you bring,
your king I'll overcome.

The night full of grief,
as I lay in my room.
Feeling numb to my relief,
weary of living in your doom.

The hate in your eyes,
your roads I've been.
Lectured of your lies,
you will not win.

Bêtise

Two lonely beings,
of mutual attraction,
exploring their feelings,
longing for affection.
Shared times are done,
haunted by memories,
our friendship now gone,
of careless pleas.

SPRING

In the meadows gracing deer,
the first day of spring is near.
Early blossoms dress the trees,
before caring their crown of leaves.
Birds in the forest chirping loudly,
flying and showing their feathers proudly.
All creatures in the shelter deep,
awaken from their winter's sleep.

GUILT IS BORN

Living in the dark,
of my cold shadow.
I'm falling apart,
to the silence below.

Smoldering guilt is born,
scorn souls are burning.
Tortured minds are worn,
quarrels are returning.

Once slaved to sin,
forced under reign.
Starving away,
from ill-gotten gain.

LONGED

Longed peace of mind,
surely within to find.
Even in the darkest night,
shines the brightest light.

MY INNERMOST

I couldn't see ahead,
blinded in what I dread.
Living in a torn world,
weathered from tears I shed.

I couldn't find my way,
stumbling along the path.
Come what may I cannot say,
no time to dwell on yesterday.

I opened my mind,
I will not surrender.
Believing all I am,
my innermost I find.

MY DEAREST CHILD

The moment you were conceived,
in my womb a precious child.
A blessing I truly believe,
my beloved too tender and mild.

My anticipation growing stronger,
as I long for you my dearest.
My love for you growing fonder,
as I hold you in my heart nearest.

The wishful day of your birth,
I admired your glowing eyes.
Welcoming you on this earth,
in my arm my babe lies.

Martina W. Mullins

You were going in a different direction,
to share your love and affection.
My hopes are too far gone,
I've been waiting for you too long.

HATE

Flaming words from a deceitful tongue,
piercing into my chest.
Anger poisoned your blood
before long.

Eyes of burning tears like fire,
of your lingering hate.
Your raging desire,
of your ill fate.

Martina W. Mullins

Hallowed thy silver moon,
in the morning hiding,
in the evening brightly shining.

Hallowed thy diamond stars bright,
glistening in the velvet sapphire night.

We often feel alone,
like a resting stone.
We often feel blue,
thing's we can't undo.

Martina W. Mullins

STORM

Canopy of gathered clouds,
cloaking the land below.
Wind of driving rush,
of a promising storm.
Golden veins strike through the air,
accompanied by raging thunder.
Surrendering rain to descent,
drenching the land beneath.

JUST ME

You don't own me,
just let me be.
We breath the air,
for us to share.
Acceptance is key,
for you and me.
Respect is mutual,
every individual.
Trust is earned,
and to be learned.
Friendship is a luxury,
between you and me.

Martina W. Mullins

CRYSTAL FOREST

Chills invading the lonesome night.
Frozen rain cloaking branches,
small and tall.
Ice glistening in the morning glow,
of the crystal forest.

IN DUE TIME

Hours gone by,
lingering thoughts,
searching for answers,
questioning why.

Days gone by,
haunting silence,
longing for truth,
us to satisfy.

Weeks gone by,
tormented minds,
hopes slowly fading,
asking why.

Months gone by,
mangled conscious,
finding reasons,
to live by.

Years gone by,
learning to accept,
making peace,
muting the cry.

Time will tell,
for us to know,
in due time,
all ends well.

SUMMER

Children chasing the babbling stream,
warm breeze flowing through their hair.
Dancing round and round,
merry songs filling the summer air.
Rosy cheeks and smiling faces,
telling secrets under the azure sky.
Puffy clouds of imaginary art,
gliding with the wind of a butterfly.

FANTASIES

Mangled thoughts of desires,
consuming my vulnerable heart.
I'm longing for your lusty flesh,
to feed my thriving hunger.
Sweet torture of erotic fantasies,
accompanying me in the lonely night.

Martina W. Mullins

UNDERSTANDING

It's only to be understood
of what we learn,
and to accept of what
we don't understand.

ANGER

Shackles cutting into my flesh,
stained with blood and anger.
Pulling these heavy chains,
of unexpressed feelings.

Martina W. Mullins

MAY NEVER BE

In lonely moments,
drifting in thoughts,
longing your presence,
dwelling on memories,
devoured in silence,
alone as before,
may never be.

CONFIDENCE

In the past while,
I'll reach out.
Validating myself,
confidence to stand trial.

All my attempts failed,
disappointed and discouraged.
Evaluating my true perception,
to secure self, unveiled.

Searching for inner strength,
to adopt new integrity.
Comprehending my limitations,
achieving with great length.

Martina W. Mullins

If you believe,
apologizing shows weakness,
than you never owned the strength,
to admit you're false.

SECRET ADMIRER

My wandering thoughts,
consuming my feeble brain.
Drawing solitary moments,
yielding to bare sane.

Your ambient eyes,
searching within to be.
Lost forever,
in a calming sea.

Your charming voice,
flicker in symphony.
Sweet words of poetry,
pouring in harmony.

My throbbing heart,
vulnerable in your sight.
Gasping for my breath,
save me, my precious delight.

Martina W. Mullins

RUNNING

Running from it all,
nothing matters anymore.
No one will find you,
hiding behind your wall.

You believe everything is lost,
shattered are your dreams.
No one guiding you through,
life treasured at your cost.

Your monster chasing you,
never ending distress.
Face your own fear,
give the demon his due.

PROCLAMATION

Tarrying in the past,
swaying my thoughts,
all I have known.

Unfulfilled ambition,
scars of insecurities,
of injured feelings.

Relinquishing bruised memories,
redeeming quarrels,
to mend my plagued mind.

Martina W. Mullins

CANDLELIGHT

Candlelight burning
in the night,
violent flickering flame,
dancing shadow on the wall.

AUTUMN

Lush foliage fading in the sun,
a new season of fall has begun.
Leaves of orange, yellow, red and green,
over mountains a vibrant blanket to be seen.
Birds of a feather flock together in the sky,
to the south for winter they must fly.
Winds blowing through branches without a care,
as withering leaves swirl in mid air.

FATE

Fear clutches my breath,
as my loved one turns into a beast.
Smothering me near death,
praying for my soul to keep.

The lives I gave birth,
guarding from this fiend.
To protect them on this earth,
no evil shall intervene.

God's consent to stow my life,
to teach and to share my love.
Whom I treasure when I'm alive,
a blessing sent from above.

FRIENDSHIP

The precious moments we spend,
the laughters and tears we share,
on each other we depend.

In the darkest hour we find the light,
together we remain strong,
overcoming with righteous might.

Many times we exchanged words,
sometimes we've disagreed,
remaining friends in our efforts.

You are my dearest friend,
enduring through tough times,
to true friendship we tend.

Martina W. Mullins

TROUBLED WATERS

Cast into the deep ocean of anguish,
I drift to the verge of despair.
Surrendering to my death wish,
the torment I no longer bare.

Troubled waters wash over me,
as the sun slowly fades away.
Swallowed into the depth of the sea,
my hope begins to decay.

Rising to the surface, I swore,
because I have one life to live.
Swimming towards the shore,
no matter what life has to give.

BROKEN PROMISE

In my waking hours I often pray,
for my love to stay.
You solemnly promised me,
your only love to be.

Unforgiving nights are long,
as I struggle to be strong.
Your are my dearest friend,
I do not wish for this to end.

Due to the haunting past,
our friendship may not last.
Whatever I may decide,
in my heart it will be right.

BELIEVE

Everyone cares for you,
even two worlds apart.
You will get through,
be strong at heart.

Save your belief,
shed no more tears.
Lasting fading grief,
departing from your fears.

LOVE ME

Captured in your eyes of lust,
your body against mine you thrust.
Your breath caressing my skin,
my blood pulsating within.
Luscious lips touching mine,
sultry tongues hungrily entwine.
Gentle hands exploring our curvy flesh,
arousal and affection mesh.
Tangled bodies dancing with erotic desire,
aching pleasures burning like fire.
In the hollow honey streams a river,
euphoria is found as my lips quiver.
Moaning passionately for you to hear,
nibbling seductively around your ear.
Feelings of driving rush in violent bliss,
as we seal our love with a sensual kiss.

MIRAGE

I'm standing in the rain,
calling your name.
Memories accompany me,
within my emotions I plea.

My heart cannot bare,
I'm a victim of time.
Whom to love I dare,
guilty of my crime.

It can never be,
between you and me.
Hindrance crossing my way,
my mind will not sway.

Courage is my victory,
morality is grounding.
My true self I must be,
confidence is bounding.

WILD CHILD

Deep pain casting my soul,
as my beloved behaves like a fool.
Each night I lay in bed crying,
weary of my wild child lying.
The restless wrongful deeds,
as my heart endlessly bleeds.
Tears streaming down my cheek,
as my fight grows weak.
I stand for my belief,
praying to free me from my grief.

Martina W. Mullins

DEPRESSION

Another lonely day struggling,
to reach the dusk.
Confined in my prison of depression,
hoping for the suffering vanishing
deep into the night.
Holding on to the last string of hope,
not falling into the emptiness below.
I'm crying out for help,
I am not heard.
Standing in the fork of the road,
uncertain which way to go.
I have faith of the purpose
of my existence,
and I'm using my last strength
to find peace within.

A DOG'S LIFE

A man's best friend they say,
full of life and full of play.
Fast paws digging holes to hide the bone,
and flower beds are never left alone.
Hunting for squirrels and cats,
and shredding their master's hats.
Strolling in the park on a sunny day,
sniffing the air and chasing the birds away.

Martina W. Mullins

A CAT'S HUNT

A cat roaming in the night,
casting a shadow in the moonlight.
Cautiously walking over the fence,
what lurks below her prey in her sense.
Motionless she turns into a beast,
to stock her helpless feast.
A squealing rodent struggling for life,
as the predator's claws filed sharp like a knife.
Her hunger satisfied at last,
finding shelter to rest.

IMMATURE HEART

One carefree soul,
making you feel beautiful.
Early love is appealing,
often as an arduous conquest.
When unable to discover, they'll vanish forever,
because of their immature heart.
Preferred long lost friend than a paramour.

GREED

One's selfishness restlessly speak,
merciless feeding from the weak.
A man's manipulation to succeed,
to satisfy their perpetual greed.

PREDETOR

In the shadow of a beast,
of feeble souls they'll feast.
Lingering silence is guilty,
beneath one's vile authority.
The longed truth shall be told,
for the vicious act to unfold.

CPSIA information can be obtained
at www.ICGtesting.com
Printed in the USA
BVHW030953050120
568584BV00001B/47/P